SOLVING PROBLEMS

Hilda Doran
Wilma McDonald
Paul Mills
Avis Swarbrick
Jim Wilson
Robert Wilson

Northern College of Education, Aberdeen

NOW! A project devised by Northern College of Education, Aberdeen
in conjunction with Occidental North Sea Consortium which comprises:
Occidental Petroleum (Caledonia) Limited
Texaco Britain Limited
International Thomson Plc
Union Texas Petroleum Limited
Published by Ward Lock Educational

Contents

Learning to Avoid Problems   *Studying instructions carefully*   3

Sub-Sea World   *Life beneath the waves*   4

Working Beneath the Sea   *The work of divers*   6

Going Deep   *Diving experiments*   8

The Diver's Gear   *Equipment for sub-sea work*   12

Silent Worlds   *Communicating without speech*   14

Floating and Sinking   *Practical problems to solve*   16

Carrying the Load   *Designing ships and boats*   18

The Story of an Oilfield   *The Claymore story*   20

Building Strong Structures   *Tubes and triangles*   22

Centre Spread   *Design to solve problems*   24

It's a Hard Life   *Alaskan adventure*   26

Friction and Lubrication   *Investigating friction*   28

Rusting Metal   *Experiments on rusting*   30

Drilling   *Finding the oil*   32

How Drilling is Done   *Getting to the oil*   34

Glorious Mud   *A solution to four problems*   37

Accidents at Work   *Looking at statistics*   38

Danger! Children at Play   *Being sensible*   39

Solving Problems   *Working in teams*   40

Working Things Out   *Talking problems over*   41

Jet Set   *A game*   42

Oil Glossary   44

Index   47

Acknowledgements   48

Learning to Avoid Problems

Being careless can cause problems at home and at school. Many problems are caused when people do not read instructions properly. Perhaps you make problems for yourself by not following instructions.

Instructions and how to read them

● Follow these instructions. Take care! There is a trick question. You will need a pencil and paper. Read *all* the questions before you start to write.
1 Write your name.
2 Write down how old you are.
3 Which of these would you find at the top of a science worksheet? – instructions about how to carry out the experiment; a list of what you need; a heading.
4 Which do you enjoy most: books of stories or books about your hobbies and interests?
5 Do not answer any question except the last.
6 Write down the purpose of this exercise.

● Give yourself a pat on the back if you avoided the trap.

When there are instructions at the top of a worksheet, always READ THEM CAREFULLY.
You must decide for yourself whether you should:
   read all the instructions before you start
   or, read a bit at a time.

● **Linemaster 25** gives examples of two kinds of worksheet. Discuss in pairs how you should read them.

● Discuss **Linemaster 25.**

● People work in different ways:
Some people want to get things done quickly.
They start without reading the instructions.
Some people read the instructions carefully and work methodically.
Some people worry so much about doing things properly that they work very slowly.
Some people find excuses not to start work at all.

● Discuss each way of working in turn.

Sub-Sea World

In many ways exploring beneath the sea is like exploring outer space. There is no air to breathe and it is cold, dark and silent. People have to travel in special vehicles if they are to stay alive. These pages help you to understand why people have explored only a small part of the **sub-sea** world.

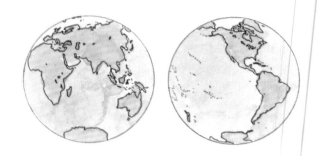

Sea covers seven tenths of the earth's surface. We have explored most of the land but only a tiny part of the ocean floor.

Journey to the bottom of the sea

If you make a journey to the bottom of the sea you will find that the sun's rays do not penetrate very far below the surface. At first every thing takes on a blue-green colour as if you were looking through blue or green tinted glasses. Lower down it becomes dark and murky. It is very cold for the water gets little heat from the sun.

As well as the cold and dark there is the weight of the water above you which presses down on your body. The further down you go, the greater this water **pressure** becomes. At a depth of 90 metres the pressure on your body will be ten times greater than it is at the surface.

Divers cannot stay down for more than a minute or two without carrying air to breathe. If they go deeper than 50 metres they must be linked to a diving vessel by a cable which carries warmth and air.

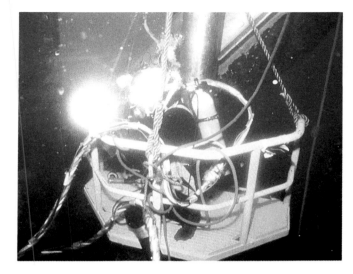

In shallow water many plants and animals live on or near the sea bed. You will find many different kinds of fish as well as crabs and lobsters. Seaweeds of different shapes and colours grow there.

At great depths things are different. Very few things live there and the bottom is sandy, stony or covered in mud.

● Compare the two photographs taken in shallow water and deep water in the sub-sea world. What life can you see in each? Make a list.
Describe the scene in each picture. Try to make the reader see and feel the difference between the two places.

● List the problems that must be overcome before people can work beneath the sea or in outer space.
Look at the divers. How does their gear help them to overcome each of these problems?

● Use the Guinness Book of Records to find out about the deepest dive man has ever made.

● Make a model sub-sea world. You will need: a cardboard box, some blue cellophane, things to decorate the inside of the box.

These questions might help. What living things might you see? What plants grow there? What might the bottom look like?

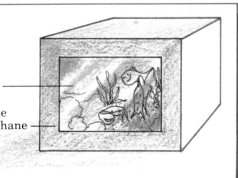

Decorate the inside of the box

View through the window of cellophane

The next pages help you to investigate some of the problems of surviving in the sea.

Working Beneath the Sea

Oil has been discovered beneath the sea bed in many parts of the world. To get the oil out **offshore platforms** are built and pipelines are laid on the sea bed.

A lot of work must be done under the sea by teams of divers. They do many important jobs such as welding pipes, installing valves at the well head and checking the safety of all the underwater structures. The divers have one of the most important and dangerous jobs in the oil industry.

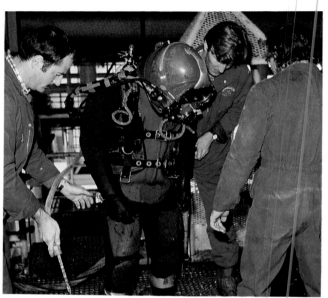

Diver in high pressure suit, attached to support ship by umbilical.

Lock out submersible. Divers live under pressure on a diving ship for up to four weeks at a time. They go down to work in a diving bell.

Submersibles

In shallow water divers can work for long periods wearing a simple diving suit and carrying two cylinders of oxygen for breathing.

For deeper work, diving bells are used. Divers descend inside the bells and go out at the required depth to do the work. They can return to the bell to rest. The bell is attached to the support ship by an **umbilical**, which is a thick cable carrying air, warmth and telephone lines. While divers are working outside the bell they wear **pressure** suits and are linked to the bell by their own umbilical. In this way they can work as deep as 400 metres.

At very great depths, divers cannot go outside the **submersible** because the pressure is too great. Work at these depths is done by robots controlled by technicians who are inside a midget submarine or on a ship on the surface of the sea.

Getting the bends

A diver coming up to the surface too quickly gets a painful disease called the **bends.** When pressure on his body reduces too fast, large gas bubbles appear throughout the diver's body and stop his blood flowing. To avoid the bends the pressure must be reduced very slowly.

When a diver has been working at a depth of 180 metres, it takes 38 hours to reduce his pressure safely. Because **decompression** takes so long, diving teams live and work under pressure for up to four weeks at a time. They enter the **hyperbaric chamber** on the diving ship at the beginning of a tour of duty. At the end of the four weeks they are slowly decompressed before going home.

Divers at work

This chart shows how divers can work at different depths.

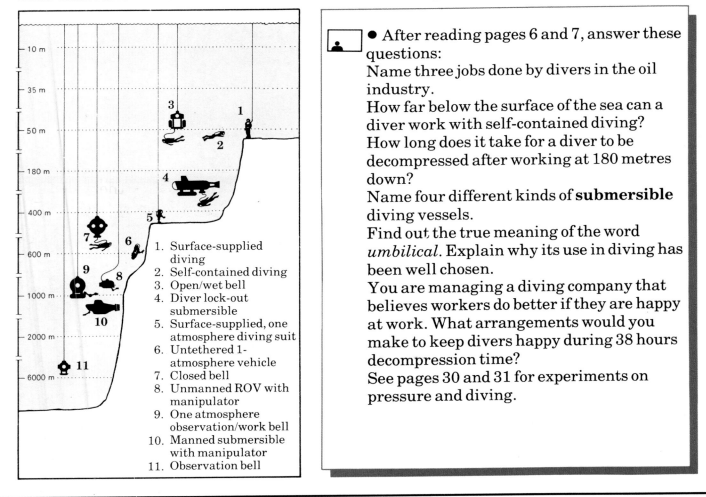

1. Surface-supplied diving
2. Self-contained diving
3. Open/wet bell
4. Diver lock-out submersible
5. Surface-supplied, one atmosphere diving suit
6. Untethered 1-atmosphere vehicle
7. Closed bell
8. Unmanned ROV with manipulator
9. One atmosphere observation/work bell
10. Manned submersible with manipulator
11. Observation bell

● After reading pages 6 and 7, answer these questions:

Name three jobs done by divers in the oil industry.

How far below the surface of the sea can a diver work with self-contained diving?

How long does it take for a diver to be decompressed after working at 180 metres down?

Name four different kinds of **submersible** diving vessels.

Find out the true meaning of the word *umbilical.* Explain why its use in diving has been well chosen.

You are managing a diving company that believes workers do better if they are happy at work. What arrangements would you make to keep divers happy during 38 hours decompression time?

See pages 30 and 31 for experiments on pressure and diving.

Going Deep

Science of diving

The problem of breathing

• Find the answers to these questions.
How long can you hold your breath?
Take 20 jumps on the spot. Now how long can you hold your breath?
How long could you stay under the sea if you did not have an air supply?

• How much air do you breathe in and out?
You will need: a large plastic bottle, some glass tubing, a cork and a measuring jug.

Fill the bottle with water. Your teacher will fix the glass tubing into the cork as shown.

Blow in at (A) for as long as you can. See how much water you can force out through (B) into the sink.

Measure the amount of water left in the bottle.
Measure the amount that the bottle holds when full.
By subtracting work out the amount of air you breathed out.

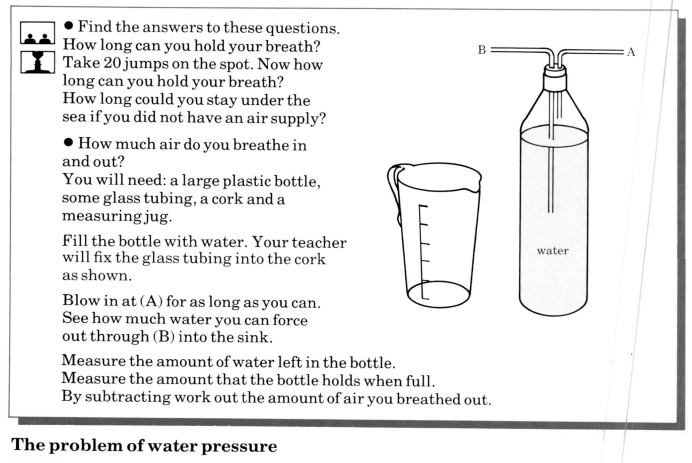

The problem of water pressure

• You will need: a tall plastic bottle, a pin.

Make holes in a straight line along the bottle

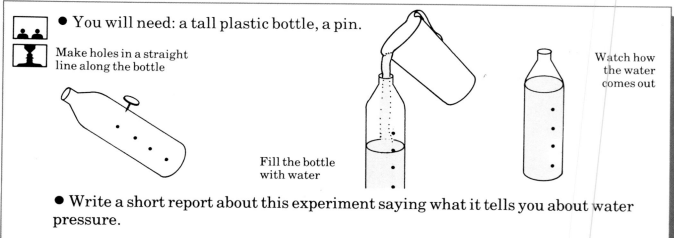

Fill the bottle with water

Watch how the water comes out

• Write a short report about this experiment saying what it tells you about water pressure.

How a diving bell works

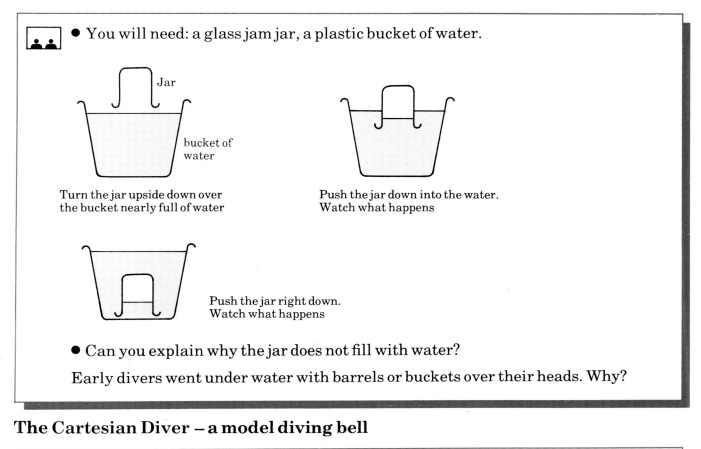

● You will need: a glass jam jar, a plastic bucket of water.

Jar

bucket of water

Turn the jar upside down over the bucket nearly full of water

Push the jar down into the water. Watch what happens

Push the jar right down. Watch what happens

● Can you explain why the jar does not fill with water?

Early divers went under water with barrels or buckets over their heads. Why?

The Cartesian Diver – a model diving bell

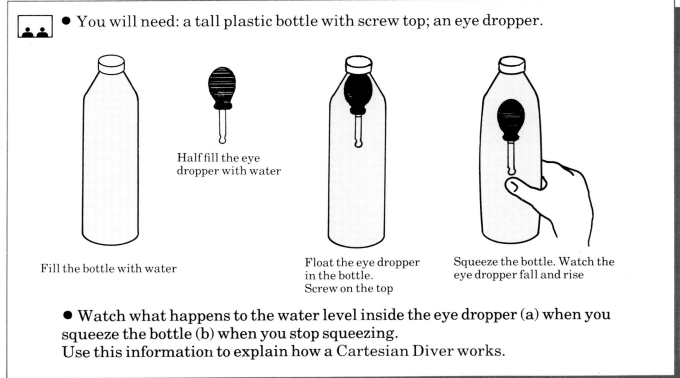

● You will need: a tall plastic bottle with screw top; an eye dropper.

Half fill the eye dropper with water

Fill the bottle with water

Float the eye dropper in the bottle. Screw on the top

Squeeze the bottle. Watch the eye dropper fall and rise

● Watch what happens to the water level inside the eye dropper (a) when you squeeze the bottle (b) when you stop squeezing.
Use this information to explain how a Cartesian Diver works.

Keeping in touch

Good communications between a diver and his **support ship** or **submersible** are very important. Divers also need to communicate clearly with each other when they are working. The sea is often dark and murky so communicating by sight can be difficult or impossible and other methods are needed. The telephone is the most convenient way of communicating between diver and support ship. The telephone wires are carried in the **umbilical** (the connecting cable between the diver and the support ship).

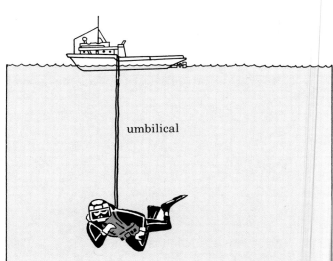

The diver keeps in touch with his support ship via a telephone link in his umbilical.

Head to head (or Tête à tête)

Divers also communicate with each other by signals and signs. They cannot talk directly to each other for sound cannot pass very easily through the water between them. However, divers whose helmets are touching can talk directly with each other, since the metal of the helmets is a good sound conductor.

Investigating sound communication

Sound conductor
Sound travels very easily through metal pipes. If you have a central heating system with radiators in your school, you can investigate a method of communicating that is often used in prisons and prison camps.

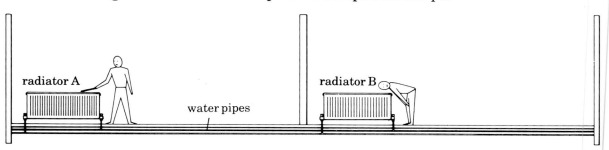

radiator A

water pipes

radiator B

Tap a radiator in one room   Listen for the sound in another

● Make up your own code (or use the Morse Code) and send a message from A to B. Can you explain how the message gets from A to B?

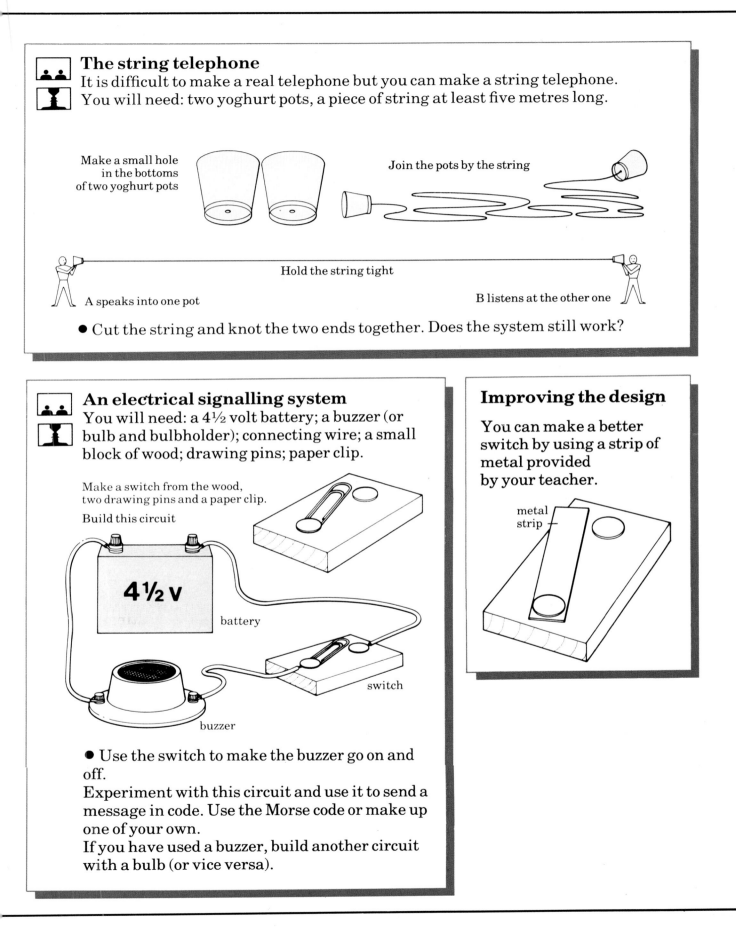

The string telephone

It is difficult to make a real telephone but you can make a string telephone.
You will need: two yoghurt pots, a piece of string at least five metres long.

Make a small hole in the bottoms of two yoghurt pots

Join the pots by the string

Hold the string tight

A speaks into one pot

B listens at the other one

- Cut the string and knot the two ends together. Does the system still work?

An electrical signalling system

You will need: a 4½ volt battery; a buzzer (or bulb and bulbholder); connecting wire; a small block of wood; drawing pins; paper clip.

Make a switch from the wood, two drawing pins and a paper clip.

Build this circuit

4½ V

battery

buzzer

switch

- Use the switch to make the buzzer go on and off.
Experiment with this circuit and use it to send a message in code. Use the Morse code or make up one of your own.
If you have used a buzzer, build another circuit with a bulb (or vice versa).

Improving the design

You can make a better switch by using a strip of metal provided by your teacher.

metal strip

The Diver's Gear

● On the opposite page is a picture of a diver in his **gear**. Parts of his gear are numbered but the labels are missing.
Read this page.
Write the numbers 1–8 in your notebook. Against each number say what the label on the diagram should be and also what problem it solves for the diver.

The problems for the diver working on the sea bed are:
— to breathe
— to keep warm
— to protect his body
— to communicate
— to move
— to stay on the sea bed while he is working.

Gear for deep sea diving

For dives deeper than 150 metres the diver wears:
— thermal underwear
— hot water suit: a loose-fitting suit containing tubes through which hot water is pumped. The hot water is pumped down from the diving ship through an **umbilical** which also carries air and communication links
— **heavy security harness** to which a cable can be attached if the diver gets into difficulties
— breast weight of several kilos
— heavy work gloves
— short working fins
— bail-out bottles of air – used to get back to diving bell in an emergency
— diving helmet fitted with earphones, microphone and valve to regulate gas for breathing

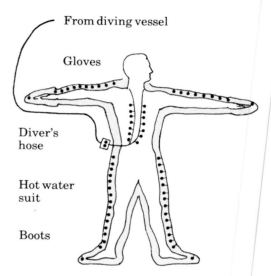

From diving vessel

Gloves

Diver's hose

Hot water suit

Boots

Shallow hot water system.

Sometimes a diver wears a diving mask. Only his face is kept completely dry. The mask is lighter than a helmet and easier to swim in.

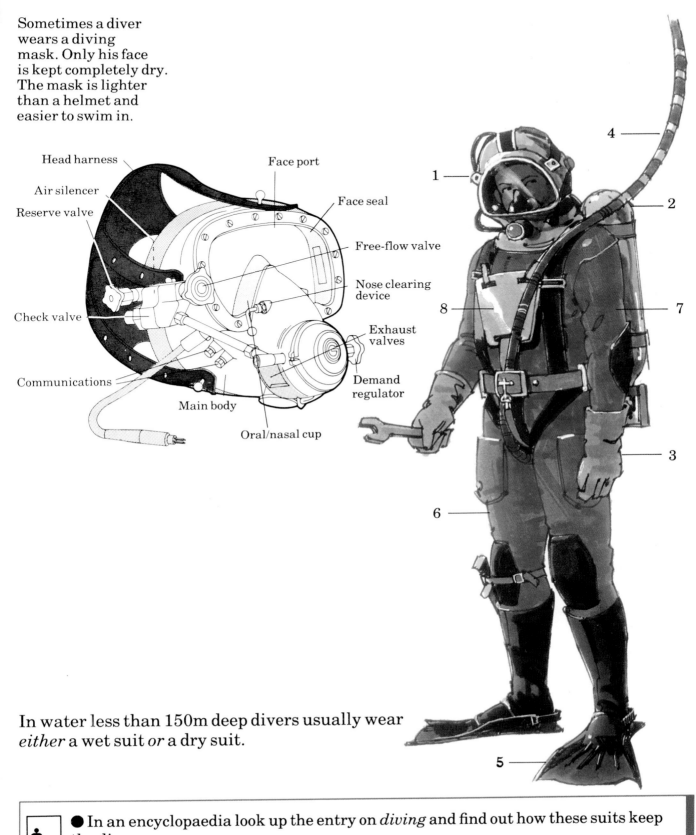

Head harness

Air silencer

Reserve valve

Check valve

Communications

Face port

Face seal

Free-flow valve

Nose clearing device

Exhaust valves

Demand regulator

Oral/nasal cup

Main body

In water less than 150m deep divers usually wear *either* a wet suit *or* a dry suit.

● In an encyclopaedia look up the entry on *diving* and find out how these suits keep the diver warm.

Silent Worlds

The world of the diver

Divers have a communication problem in the sub-sea world. When they cannot talk to each other divers communicate by signs. Here are some of the signs they use.

Hand signals

I have no more air

I am low on air

I am out of breath

Stop Stay where you are

OK? Is all well?

Go up Go down

You OR me

Something wrong

Distress

- In pairs make up a conversation in signs in which one diver tells another he is short of air. They decide to go up to the surface together.

- Imagine one of you has found something on the sea bed. Tell the other about it in signs. Act your conversation to the class who will interpret your story.

Line signals

When divers are connected to a support vessel by a line they can communicate by tugging on the line.
A strong firm pull is called a *pull*.
A short sharp tug is called a *bell*.

- Join up in pairs. Stretch a piece of string between you. Use the signals to send a silent message.

GENERAL SIGNALS

Signal	Tender	Diver
ONE PULL	To call attention. Are you OK?	To call attention. I am OK. Arrived or left bottom.
TWO PULLS	Am sending down a rope.	Send down a rope.
THREE PULLS	You have come up too far. Go down slowly until I stop you.	I am going down.
FOUR PULLS SUCCESSION OF PULLS (More than four)	Come up. Emergency signal. Come up immediately.	May I come up? Emergency signal. Pull me up immediately.
FOUR PULLS– TWO BELLS	Come up. Hurry up. Come up – surface D/C.	I want to come up. Assist me up.
SUCCESSION OF TWO BELLS		Am foul and need assistance.
SUCCESSION OF THREE BELLS		Am foul but can clear myself.

Sign languages

Deaf people live in a silent world. They communicate by signs. Here are some of the signs they use.

1. CAN'T
   Trace a cancelling-out mark. Do this with both hands emphatically for 'Impossible'.

2. COME

3. HELP
   Put flat hand under 'heavy' flat to help lift it.

4. HOW MANY?
   Wiggle and move away from mouth.

5. LITTLE

6. LONG
   Use index finger to trace long line up arm.

- Make up a conversation. You can invent more signs if you like.
- Act out your conversation to the class.
- Did you find anything difficult to say in sign language?
- Make a list of problems that deaf people face.

Finger spelling alphabet

Deaf people use this alphabet. You can find out about it by writing to:
The Royal National Institute for the Deaf, 105, Gower Street, London WC1.

- Find out other ways of sending silent messages, for example semaphore or how bookies communicate at race courses.

Floating and Sinking

In June 1976 the completed Claymore jacket was pushed off the slipway at Cherbourg harbour on to a waiting 150 metre barge. The sea voyage to its location in the North Sea took two days.

At that point the empty **ballast tanks** at the front of the barge were filled with water. The barge tilted forward and 10 000 tonnes of steel slid with a grating screech into the North Sea. The giant steel jacket came to rest on its side, kept afloat by **buoyancy bottles** attached to its legs. The bottles were carefully flooded with water. The jacket swung to the vertical, floating with its base 6 metres above the sea bed.

Tugs pulled the jacket into position. More water let into the buoyancy bottles and the jacket began settling into the mud. Hammering of the 50 metre long steel **piles** began immediately and was completed within a month.

Some floating and sinking problems

On your mark!

- You will need: a bottle, a coin, sink of water.

- Put coin on the bottom of a sink. Fill the sink with water. Your task is to add water gradually to the bottle so that it will sink vertically on top of the coin.

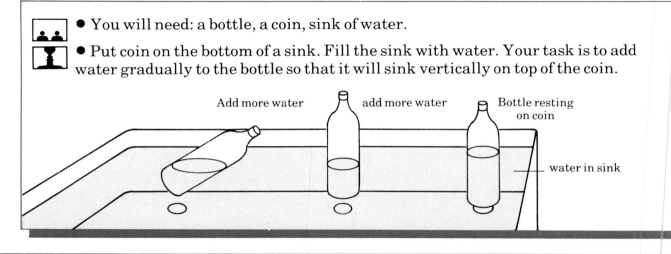

Add more water   add more water   Bottle resting on coin

water in sink

A Question of Buoyancy

- Plasticine usually sinks in water. Can you find a way of (a) making it float on the surface and (b) suspending it half way between the surface and the bottom?

- You will need: 100 gramme lump of plasticine, thread, a piece of polystyrene. In your project notebook, draw sketches to show how you solved this problem.

Floaters
- You will need: a polybag, 4 pipe cleaners, 2 empty match boxes, a 200 gramme mass, a sink full of water.

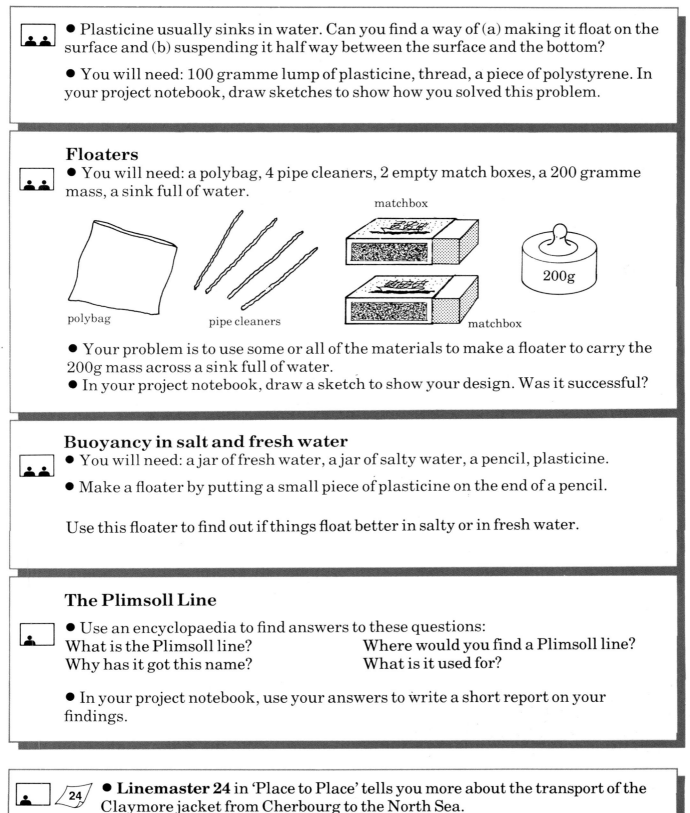

matchbox

polybag   pipe cleaners   matchbox   200g

- Your problem is to use some or all of the materials to make a floater to carry the 200g mass across a sink full of water.
- In your project notebook, draw a sketch to show your design. Was it successful?

Buoyancy in salt and fresh water
- You will need: a jar of fresh water, a jar of salty water, a pencil, plasticine.

- Make a floater by putting a small piece of plasticine on the end of a pencil.

Use this floater to find out if things float better in salty or in fresh water.

The Plimsoll Line

- Use an encyclopaedia to find answers to these questions:
What is the Plimsoll line?   Where would you find a Plimsoll line?
Why has it got this name?   What is it used for?

- In your project notebook, use your answers to write a short report on your findings.

- **Linemaster 24** in 'Place to Place' tells you more about the transport of the Claymore jacket from Cherbourg to the North Sea.

Carrying the Load

Different vessels are built to do different jobs.

- Look at the vessels in the photographs below. For *each* vessel do the following:

- Sketch the shape as if you were looking down on it from the air – is it long and narrow or short and wide?
Does it have a helideck? If so add it to your sketch.

- Next sketch its shape as if you were looking at it from another ship. How many decks has it? Can you see cranes and other tall objects sticking up – if so put them in.

- Beside each sketch say what you think the vessel is used for.

- When you have finished, use **Linemaster 26** to check your answers.

Semi-submersible drilling rigs

These vessels are used for drilling in deep water. They float on large tanks of air called pontoons.

The drill string goes down through the sea to the sea bed. Special equipment is used to stop the drill string snapping off when the vessel sways from side to side or goes up and down with wind and tide.

 ● Design a raft that will float on four plastic bottles. See how much weight the raft will carry without sinking.

Build a paper raft

Your problem is to find out what shape of raft will carry the greatest load.

You will need: a bag of marbles, sellotape, two pieces of stiff paper 10 × 8 cm marked as shown in the diagram, a sink full of water.

● Fold the papers along the dotted lines. Cut the corners and stick them with sellotape to make rafts as shown. Float your rafts in a sink of water.

● How many marbles do you have to put in the raft to make it sink?

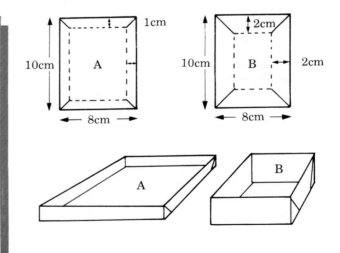

● Try making rafts of other shapes but still using the same area of paper.
● Predict which raft you think will hold the most marbles.
● Test your prediction.
● Write a report of your experiment giving results.
● Write down what this experiment tells you about the different shapes of the vessels on the opposite page.

The Story of an Oilfield

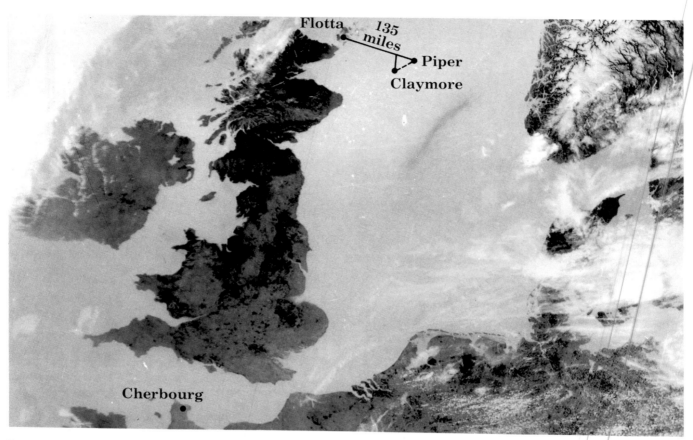

Flotta • 135 miles

• Piper

Claymore

Cherbourg •

In May 1974 a large **oilfield** was discovered in the North Sea. It was named the Claymore Field. It lies to the north-east of Scotland and is shown on this map which was made using a satellite photograph. Before the oil could be recovered, a **production platform** had to be designed, built and taken to the correct place.

This posed several problems.

In that area the sea is 110m deep. The equipment had to be held 40 metres above the waves. Therefore a very *large* structure was needed.

The machinery and living quarters would weigh 20 000 tonnes, and the legs (called the **jacket**) would weigh another 10 000 tonnes. Therefore the structure had to be very *strong*.

Finally it had to be put up in exactly the right place. Huge waves and gale-force winds might make this difficult.

The jacket was built at Cherbourg in France. In June 1976 it was towed out to the North Sea and was fixed by hammering long steel rods called **piles** into the sea bed. The rest of the equipment had already been built and was taken out and hoisted on to the jacket.

In November 1977 the first oil flowed from the Claymore Field through an undersea pipeline to Flotta in Orkney.

Read the story on the opposite page and answer these questions

- List the three most important problems that had to be solved by the engineers designing the Claymore platform.

- Look at the satellite map. Estimate how far the jacket had to be towed from Cherbourg to Claymore.

It took two days to complete the journey. What was the average speed?

Bigger and bigger

Drilling for oil under the sea began in 1947.

The first attempts took place in shallow water near the shore. As the engineering and design problems were overcome, drilling rigs and platforms moved out into deeper waters.

This diagram shows how production jackets grew bigger and stronger as oil-fields were discovered in deeper and deeper parts of the sea.

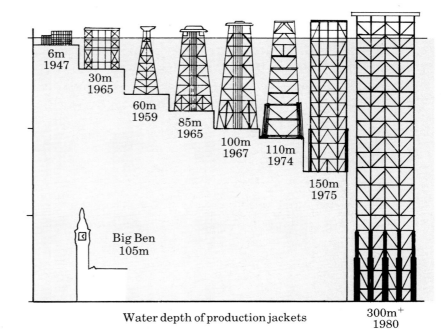

Water depth of production jackets

Look at the diagram and then answer these questions:

- After 1947, how many years passed before engineers could build a jacket strong enough to stand in 300m of water?

- A football pitch is about 90m long. How many of the production jackets in the diagram are taller than the length of a football pitch?

- The three biggest jackets have very thick legs at the bottom. Can you think of an explanation for this?

- All the jackets are slightly different yet all have one shape in common. This shape is very important in designing strong structures. What shape do all these jackets have in common?

- Find the Claymore production jacket on the diagram on this page. Sketch it in your notebook. Add the following to your sketch: depth of sea and weight of equipment. Make your sketch more real by drawing waves and stormy weather.

Building Strong Structures

Pages 20 and 21 describe the problems of building **production platforms** to be placed in the North Sea. They must be strong enough to carry great weights and to stand up to winter storms. They must also be light enough to be transported to the oil field and they must not collapse under their own weight.

Engineers and designers have found that two things in particular will make structures both very strong and very light. Firstly, the *triangle* is the most rigid shape we know. Secondly, *hollow tubes* are about as strong as solid ones and are easily transported and handled.

Investigating shapes

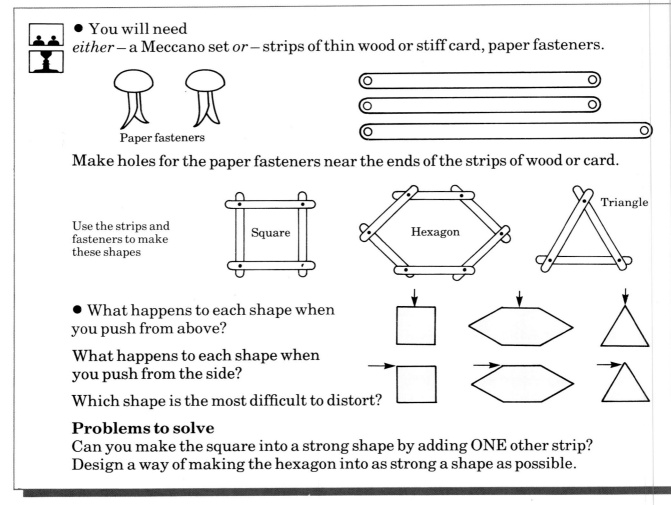

- You will need
either – a Meccano set *or* – strips of thin wood or stiff card, paper fasteners.

Paper fasteners

Make holes for the paper fasteners near the ends of the strips of wood or card.

Use the strips and fasteners to make these shapes

Square

Hexagon

Triangle

- What happens to each shape when you push from above?

What happens to each shape when you push from the side?

Which shape is the most difficult to distort?

Problems to solve
Can you make the square into a strong shape by adding ONE other strip?
Design a way of making the hexagon into as strong a shape as possible.

Investigating tubes

● You will need: some sheets of A4 paper, scissors, glue, large weights, a weight hanger.

How strong is a paper tube?
Are tubes of large diameter stronger than tubes of small diameter?

● Make three tubes of the SAME material and length but of DIFFERENT diameters . . . .

Cut out three strips of paper like these

Roll them into tubes and glue down the edges

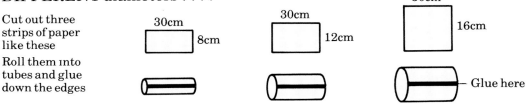

● Which tube do you think will be strongest? Make a note.

Hang weights from each tube to see how much each one can support

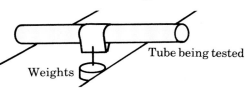

Weights   Tube being tested

Which tube was the strongest? Present your results in a bar graph.
Was your prediction about the strongest tube correct?
Write a report of your investigation.

How much weight can vertical tubes support?
● Make three tubes of the SAME material and length but of DIFFERENT diameters.

Cut out three strips of paper like these and roll them into tubes

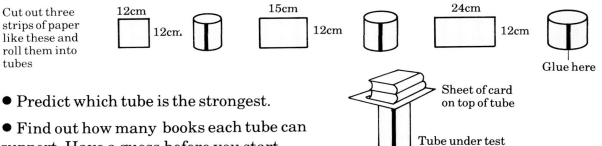

Sheet of card on top of tube

Tube under test

● Predict which tube is the strongest.

● Find out how many books each tube can support. Have a guess before you start.

Which tube supported the greatest weight? Present your results as a bar graph.
Write a report of this experiment. Remember to include your prediction.

Two challenging problems
● You will need: lots of newspaper, sellotape – and that's all!

Use your knowledge of strong structures to build a structure 1.5 metres high which can support a weight of at least 1 kg.
Build a bridge between two tables that is strong enough to support the weight of your teacher.

Larger and smaller

In the last 20 years bigger and bigger structures have been built for industry. They are needed to find and produce oil and gas under deep seas far from land. At the same time computers have become smaller and more powerful. They have been used in designing these giant structures. They help to keep them running. Every year brings new ideas and new inventions. We live in a rapidly changing world.

Tension leg platform: Hutton field.

Concrete gravity platform: Ninian field.

Semi-submersible drilling rig.

Satellite production module: Scapa field.

...ill ship.

Land-based drilling rig.

...ck-up rig.

Steel production platform: Claymore field.

 ● Each of the rigs and platforms shown on these pages was designed to solve a particular problem. Use the glossary to find out about the problem.

● Find out how computers are used in your school.

● Find out how computers are used at the local petrol station, or in a local business.

 ● In the next 20 years many other problems will be solved. There will be many new inventions. Use your imagination to write your account of what life will be like then. Illustrate it. Make your story interesting and exciting.

It's a Hard Life!

When people have to live and work in places where the climate is harsh or uncomfortable we say they are in a *hostile environment*.

Here is what oil companies had to face when they started working in the very cold environment of Alaska.

The biggest oilfield in the USA is at Prudhoe Bay in northern Alaska.

In winter the sun does not rise above the horizon for 56 days. The cold is intense. The wind sweeps the snow into great drifts and the temperature can drop to −80°C.

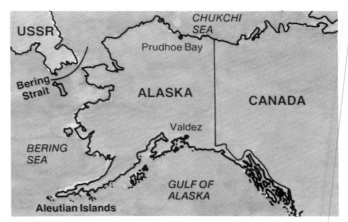

Alaska is vast. It is larger than Britain, France, Italy and Spain all put together.

● Here are eight problems. Read about them then take **Linemaster 27**. The solutions are mixed up. Cut along the dotted lines and match them to the problems below.

1. Uncovered human flesh can freeze in seconds.
2. Buildings can be cold and dark all day.
3. Metal becomes brittle and can shatter like glass.
4. Lubricants freeze in the machinery.
5. The sea is completely frozen over except for six weeks in summer when the ice moves away from the shore.

6. The ground is frozen to a depth of 600m. This is called *permafrost*. The hot oil coming out of the ground could melt the permafrost and the platform would sink.

7. The *permafrost* is protected by a mat of moss, lichen and grass. In summer when the top layer melts it becomes soggy and can be easily destroyed by walking or driving on it.

8. Platforms and rigs become covered with a very heavy, thick layer of ice.

27 • Complete the chart on daylight and darkness on **Linemaster 27**.

Laying the pipeline

A pipeline 1284 km long takes the oil from Prudhoe Bay in the north to the ice-free port of Valdez in the south.

640 km of the pipeline is above ground on stilts.

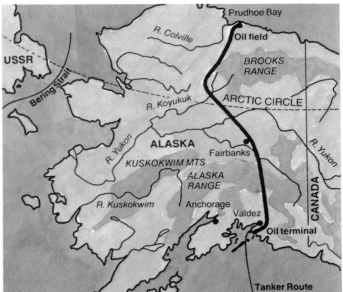

• What problems had to be solved when this pipeline was built?
Study the pictures and the map above.

Friction and Lubrication

Have you ever wondered why gym shoes have rubber or synthetic soles? Do you slip more easily if the gym floor is wet? The force that stops you slipping is called **friction**.

Finding out about friction

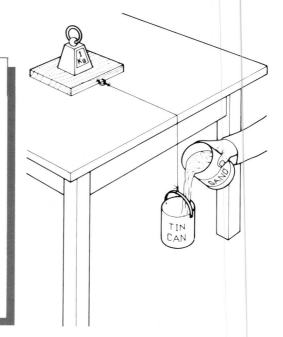

● Attach a string to a hook on a block of wood, and tie a can on to the other end. Put a 1kg weight on top of the wood. Then pour sand into the can until the wood just starts to slide. Weigh the amount of sand you put in the can. How much sand did you have to add? What happens if you repeat the investigation with a 2kg weight on the wood?

If you need a lot of sand to make the block of wood slide, then the friction is *high*. If you need a little sand to make the block of wood slide then the friction is *low*.

● Repeat the investigation but this time put some water on the table under the block.

Does this make any difference to the friction?

Any substance that reduces friction is called a **lubricant**. A lubricant makes things slip more easily. In this case water is a lubricant.

Reducing friction
In the old days when wooden drawers kept sticking they were rubbed with candle wax. This made them slide more easily.

Candle wax is a good lubricant for wood. If water had been used it would have soaked into the wood. Would water then act as a lubricant?

You need to match the kind of lubricant which is used to the kinds of surfaces which are sliding over one another.

Oil is a good lubricant for metal surfaces.
Why do you think this is?
Think about what it must be like inside an engine with hot metal surfaces sliding over one another.
The oil has to stop them from rubbing together.
It has to be a very special mixture to stand up to those conditions.

What happens when you rub handcream onto your hands when they are rough and dry?
Is the handcream a lubricant?

● Find out how you lubricate a fishing line.

Friction on a bike and its lubrication

● In this picture of a bike, certain parts have been numbered 1–10. Copy out the table. Say whether each part should have high or low friction. Which parts should be lubricated with oil?

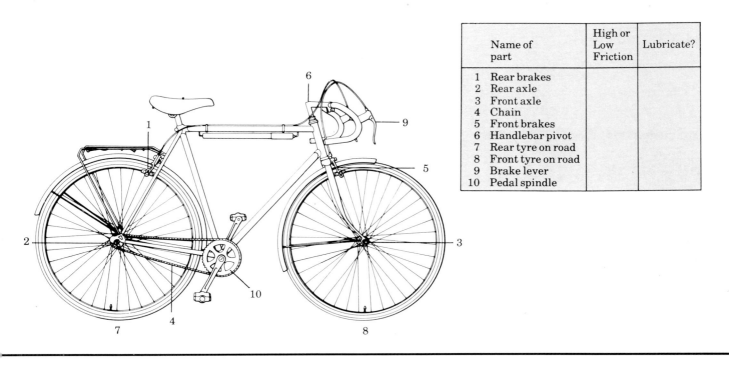

Name of part	High or Low Friction	Lubricate?
1 Rear brakes		
2 Rear axle		
3 Front axle		
4 Chain		
5 Front brakes		
6 Handlebar pivot		
7 Rear tyre on road		
8 Front tyre on road		
9 Brake lever		
10 Pedal spindle		

Rusting Metal

How many times have you heard people grumbling
about car bodies or exhaust pipes going rusty?
You may have tried to clean rust off a bicycle.

The following tests will help you to discover what makes
metal go rusty.

- You will need two jars, two similar nails and some water.
  Put one of the nails in a jar of air, and the other one in a jar full of water.
  Leave them for at least a week.
  Which nail goes rusty?
  What does rust look like?

- Write a short account about what you did, and what you found out.

Air in water

Water contains lots of air.
1. If you boil water, all the air is driven out of it.
2. If you then cover the surface of the water with a thin layer of oil, no air can get
   back into the water.

- Use these two facts to design a fair test using two other nails to see if the air in
  water helps rust to form.
  Which nail went rusty first this time? Add this to your account.

Salt in water

In winter we put down tons of salt on our roads when it
is snowy or icy. Perhaps this makes rusting worse on
our cars and lorries.

- Make up a test to see if salt water causes more rusting than fresh water.
  Add the results to your account.

Rustproofing

Metals can be protected to stop them from going rusty.
Motor car manufacturers try very hard to stop rust.

 ● Ask a local car dealer for a catalogue describing one of the new cars he sells. Look at the information the catalogue gives about the rust proofing of both the upper and undersides of the car.

● Make up your own test to investigate ways of stopping nails from rusting in sea water. Add the results to your account.

Here are some clues.
You could try smearing the nails with grease or oil, or painting them, or smearing them with car underseal.

Rust at sea

Jacob's Dad works on an oil platform which is made of metal tubes. He says that rusting is worst on the legs just at sea level.

● Design a test to investigate this, using nails and sea water or salt water.
What did you find?
Can you think of a reason for this?
Add the test and your findings to your account.

Look at all the things you have found out about rusting in these tests.

● Write an account for your teacher or give a short talk to the rest of the class about rusting metals.
● Make some drawings or paintings to illustrate your account or talk.

Drilling

Where shall we drill?

This map shows where oil or gas might be found in the British Isles. It has been made by **geologists** and **geophysicists**, whose job is to investigate rocks below the surface of the ground.

Before oil companies drill a hole, they ask geologists to pin-point places where petroleum might be trapped – it is not found everywhere. Geologists do this by making a **seismic survey**.

Read about this and answer the questions on the next page.

Seismic surveys
If there is a seismic survey in your area, you will see a series of trucks and big vehicles on the road. They are linked by cables. A notice in the local paper will tell you when a survey will take place.

The white truck is making a vibrating sound. You can feel the ground trembling. The vibrations go down into the ground and bounce back from the rocks below.

The **geophones** in this photograph are like microphones. They pick up the vibrations bouncing back from the rock layers.

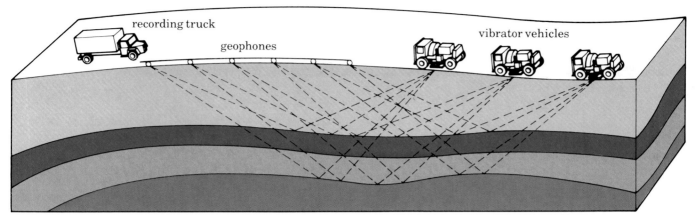

recording truck

geophones

vibrator vehicles

*A recording truck records the data. Computers back in the office make a **print-out** which shows the different rock layers.*

The geophysicists in the photograph are examining a print-out from a seismic survey. They are hoping to find places where oil or gas might be trapped. Oil is trapped by folds and faults in underground rocks, so they will be looking for signs of these. Of course they cannot be certain. Only about 1 in 10 wild cat wells shows enough oil to make production worth while.

Answer these questions:
- Put these stages of a seismic survey in the right order:
the recording truck makes a tape-recording of the vibrations;
the vibrations travel down through the ground and bounce back from layers of rock;
a truck makes a vibrating noise;
computers turn the recordings into a print-out showing the different rock layers;
geophones pick up the vibrations and send them to the recording truck.

Look at the diagram at the top of the page.
- Which vibrations would reach a geophone first — those bouncing off the top or the bottom layer of rock? Can you explain why?
(hint: vibrations travel at the same speed through rocks).
- How would you know whether there was going to be a seismic survey near your school?
- Sketch a vibrator vehicle and a geophone. (Use the photographs and diagrams to get ideas.)
- For millions of years bats have been finding their way in the dark by bouncing sound off the things around them. Industry and medicine now use the same idea. Look up *ultrasonics* in a good encyclopaedia. Skim the article and list as many uses of ultrasound as you can find (there is no need to read every word.)

- Make some drawings or paintings to illustrate your account or talk

How Drilling is Done

Drilling a well

Oil, gas and water lie trapped in rocks
under the ground.
Drilling is the only way to get them out.
A drill works like this: a motor turns a **bit**.
The bit drills a hole.
Oil rigs may make holes two or three miles
deep — or even more.

Oil rigs

The **drill bit** is screwed into a 9 metre long
drill pipe. Different bits are used for
different rocks. They have very hard teeth,
sometimes made of diamonds or tungsten
carbide.

As it turns, the bit grinds a hole through
the rock and slowly sinks. Eventually
another length of drill pipe must be screwed
on. As more and more pipes are added the
drill string lengthens.

When the drill bit wears out it must be
changed. Doing this is called a **round trip**.
All the drill pipes are pulled out of the hole
three at a time and stacked in the derrick.
This can take several hours if the well is
deep.

The drill bit is changed. The pipes are put
back in the hole three at a time. At last the
drill bit touches the bottom of the hole
again, and drilling can start once more.

> ● **Linemaster 28** is a diagram of a
> drilling rig. Fill it in and keep it
> beside you as you read pages 35–39.

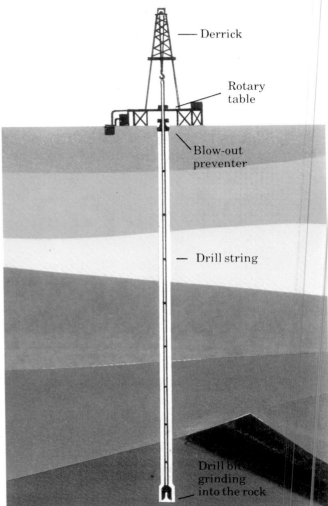

— Derrick

Rotary
table

Blow-out
preventer

— Drill string

Drill bit
grinding
into the rock

This photograph shows two **roughnecks** at work. They are using big handling grabs to grip two drill pipes while they screw them together.

Next they will release the grabs and swing them out of the way. They will bend down and take away the clamps on the floor that hold the bottom drill pipe in place. The pipes will be lowered through the hole.

The wheel on the floor will grip the top drill pipe and start to spin round. It turns the whole drill string with the drill bit at the bottom.

Roughnecks have two main jobs. They add extra drill pipes as the well gets deeper, and they pull out and replace all the pipes when the bit has to be changed. It is hard and dirty work. They work 12 hour shifts. Their busiest time is during a round trip.

- Write down the two main jobs of a roughneck.
- Write down the three stages of a round trip.
- Drill pipes are pulled out in 27 metre lengths, called *stands*.
  How many drill pipes are there in a stand?
- How many stands would be brought out of a well 2700m deep?
- If the roughnecks worked hard and saved 30 seconds on each stand, how much time would they save on that round trip?
  If running a drilling rig cost £72,000 a day, how much money would they save?

- When the roughnecks screw drill pipes together, or unscrew them, they use large spanners called handling grabs. Work out a way of showing that a spanner can make a tighter joint than you can make with your hands.

The cutting edge

The photograph shows two drillers looking at a drill bit. It has just been brought up from hundreds of metres below the ground, where it was drilling a hole through a layer of rock.

- Make a sketch of the drill bit and the *pipe above it*. The drill bit is at the bottom. Label it.
- Work out the diameter of the drill bit at its widest (roughly). Do it like this:
a) with your ruler measure on the photograph the diameter of the drill bit.
b) with your ruler measure on the photograph the distance between a man's elbow and the end of his fingers. On a man this usually measures about 45cm.
You should now be able to work out the approximate diameter of the drill bit, and therefore the diameter of the hole it makes. Note this information on your sketch.
- Above the bit is a pipe with a bulge in it. This is called the drill collar. It is heavy and thick to force the drill bit through the rock. Label the drill collar on your sketch.
- Look at the photographs on this page and on page 33. List four pieces of protective clothing worn by the workers. Opposite each write down why you think it is necessary.

Problem solving
- Work out a way of showing that a drill bit gets hot when it is drilling. (How did cave men make fire?)
- Work out a way of showing that the drill bit must be harder than the rock it is cutting through.
Hint: you could use a wooden skewer and a metal skewer, a wooden board and a metal sheet. Explain what this has to do with diamond drill bits.

Glorious Mud

A drill bit spins round hundreds of times a minute. In the early days of drilling this caused problems. The drill bit got very hot. Chips of rock clogged the hole. You could not tell what kind of rock was being drilled or whether it had oil in it. Four problems.

Finally engineers worked out a simple solution that dealt with all four problems at the same time: MUD!

Not quite like the mud you see in a puddle. The glossary at the end of this book tells you what this mud is like.

Mud is pumped down the centre of the drill string, it comes out through the drill bit and back up between the drill string and the wall of the well.

It cools and lubricates the bit. It washes away chippings and brings them to the surface. There the chippings can be examined to see what kind of rock is

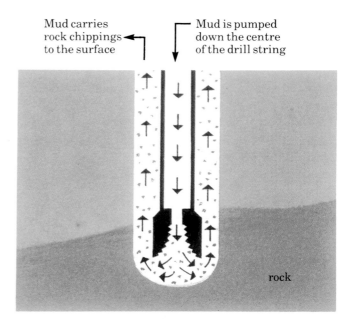

Mud carries rock chippings to the surface

Mud is pumped down the centre of the drill string

rock

being drilled and if it has oil in it.

But mud does even more than this. It stops walls of the well caving in and helps to prevent a blow-out.

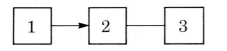

● Two methods of note-taking are described below. Decide which would be the better one for making notes on *Drilling problems and solutions*. When you have made notes, use them to write a report.

a) Flow chart – used to show the order in which things happen.

1 → 2 → 3

b) Tabulation – used to collect facts under headings.

	Heading	Heading
1		
2		
3		

● If you were making notes on a **round trip** (page 34) would you use a flow chart or tabulation? Explain why.

Accidents at Work

Few people get through the whole of their working lives without being involved in some sort of accident at work. Some jobs are much safer to do than others, and some workplaces are more safe than others. Set out below is a possible, but made-up, accident record of an industry for one particular year. Study the information, and then answer the questions.

Number of Accidents During One Year in an Industry

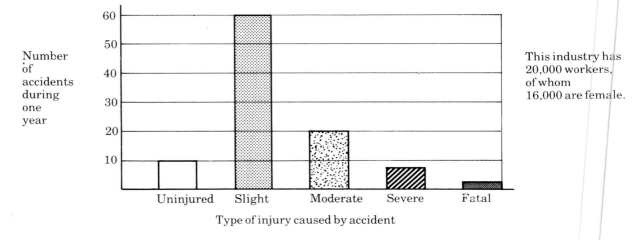

This industry has 20,000 workers, of whom 16,000 are female.

Type of injury caused by accident

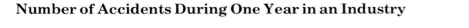

- Match the type of injury with the proper description (they are jumbled up).

Type	Description of Injury Caused by the Accident
Uninjured	Requiring a stay in hospital and a long time off work
Slight	Resulting in the worker's death
Moderate	No injuries were sustained
Severe	Requiring first aid but worker able to continue working
Fatal	Requiring hospital treatment and a few days off work

- How many men are employed in the industry?
- What is the total number of accidents that occurred in the year shown?
- In that year, only 75 workers were involved in accidents. What does this fact tell you about some of the workers who were involved in accidents during the year?
- How many workers were not involved in accidents during the year?
- Of the accidents that did happen, 50% of them happened to female workers. How many accidents happened to female workers?
- How many accidents happened to male workers?

Danger! Children at Play

Look carefully at these pictures.

There's only me between you and the farmyard.

This place looks as if it would be fun to explore!

I've just slipped away for a bit of quiet fishing.

- What sort of accidents do you think might happen to children who ventured into the places shown above?
- What sorts of accidents might lead to fatal injuries for children in those places?

Accidents at school

- Schools are places of work. Name three other sorts of job that are done in schools besides teaching.

Accidents sometimes happen in schools, and sometimes children cause them to happen.

Do you ever run along corridors and around 'blind' corners?
help to make icy slides in playgrounds in winter?
leave your belongings where other people can trip over them?
forget to tie your shoelaces?
leave taps running?
rush to be first into or out of the classroom?

- Design a poster, setting out 'DO's' and 'DON'T's' for pupils as part of a 'Make School a Safer Place' campaign.
You can use the 'DON'T's' listed above, and try and think of some other 'DO's' and 'DON'T's' to include.

Solving Problems

Difficulties often arise when people have to work together as a team to do a job. Here is an opportunity for you to learn how to deal with some of these difficulties.

Working in *threes* or *fours* you are going to produce *one* of the following about one part of this term's work –
- a picture or a collage with notes
- an illustrated presentation for your own or another class
- an illustrated newspaper report
- a slide-tape programme
- a dramatisation

When you have made up your team you will have to decide:
1. Exactly what you mean to do. Write this down in your book.
2. Whether you want to choose a leader.
3. What equipment you will need. List this in your book.
4. What each person's job is going to be.

Discuss your plans with your teacher. Ask her to tell you how much time you have to complete the task.
Now plan a programme of work that fits in with this time scale.
Complete your task.
When you have completely finished your task do **Linemaster 29** as a group.

Working Things Out

Many of our difficulties come from our relationships with other people.
Sometimes we don't want to do things they want us to do.
Sometimes we want to do things they don't want us to do.

Here are some children who think they have problems. Perhaps the families think they have problems too!

● Dramatise the situations and try to work through the problems.

Sally would like to get a brand new sports outfit in the latest fashion. Mother says they cannot afford it. Sally is continually nagging and quarrelling. The rest of the family are tired of her complaining. They all discuss the problem.

Kim is very untidy. He leaves things lying about all over the house. He spends all his spare time watching TV. He refuses to help with the housework. The family decide something must be done about it.

David and Cari have ganged up against one of their former friends, who is afraid to come to school. The head teacher has invited the parents of all three children to come to school to discuss the problem.

Jet-Set

A time game for 2 to 4 pairs of players.
You will need a dice, coloured counters and copies of Linemaster 30.

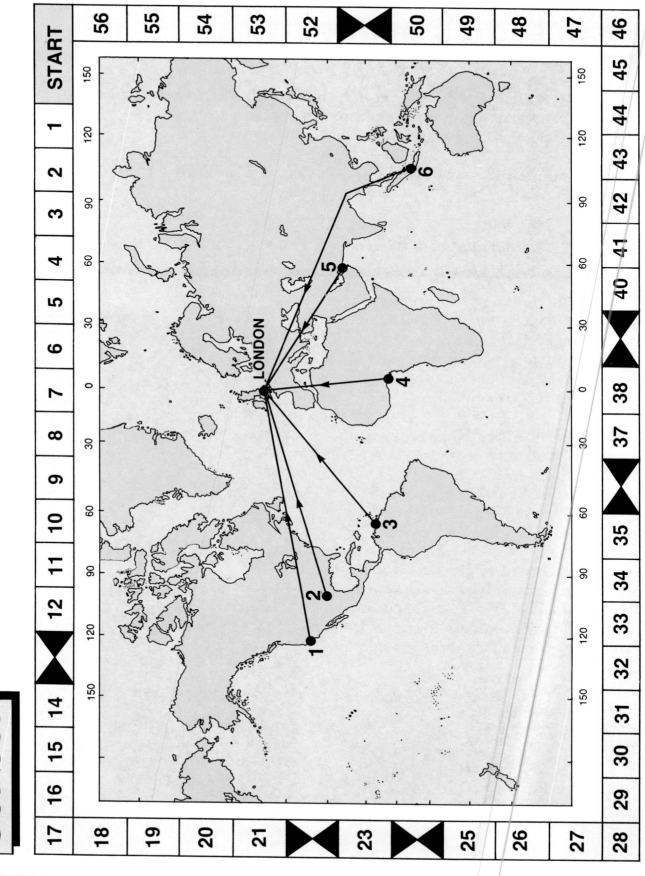

Urgent message! Return to London Head Office as soon as possible.

Shake dice for *LOCATION and TIMETABLE INFORMATION*.

Shake dice again for *FLIGHT INFORMATION*. Fill up a *TIME SHEET* for London Head Office.

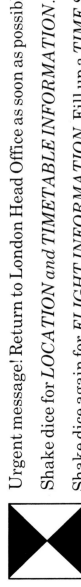

LOCATION INFORMATION

Die	Location
1	Los Angeles / California U.S.A. / 8 hours time difference
2	Houston / Texas U.S.A. / 6 hours time difference
3	Caracas / Venezuela South America / 4 hours time difference
4	Lagos / Nigeria. Africa / 1 hour time difference
5	Dubai / Persian Gulf / 4 hours time difference
6	Jakarta / Java. Indonesia / 7 hours time difference

LOCATION INFORMATION (TIMETABLE)

Los Angeles to London
Depart ☐ 17.30 ☐ 20.00
Arrive ☐ 03.40 ☐ 07.10
Add 8 hours to flight time

Houston to London
Depart ☐ 18.00 ☐ 19.10 ☐ 20.00
Arrive ☐ 03.00 ☐ 04.10 ☐ 05.00
Add 6 hours to flight time

Caracas to London
Depart ☐ 20.50 ☐ 21.35
Arrive ☐ 08.19 ☐ 09.00
Add 4 hours to flight time

Lagos to London
Depart ☐ 09.30 ☐ 12.00
Arrive ☐ 16.25 ☐ 18.55
Subtract 1 hour from flight time

Dubai to London
Depart ☐ 09.00 ☐ 23.00
Arrive ☐ 19.45 ☐ 09.45
Subtract 4 hours from flight time

Jakarta to London
Depart ☐ 22.10
Arrive ☐ 13.45
Subtract 7 hours from flight time

LOCATION INFORMATION (FLIGHT)

Die	Flight Information
1	First flight booked up. Take next available flight out. Penalty – add 2 hours on
2	No delay. No penalty
3	Fog delays take-off. Penalty – add 2 hours
4	Luggage lost on arrival in London. Penalty – add 1 hour
5	Traffic Controllers' strike at London. Plane diverted to Manchester. Penalty – add 4 hours
6	No delay. No penalty

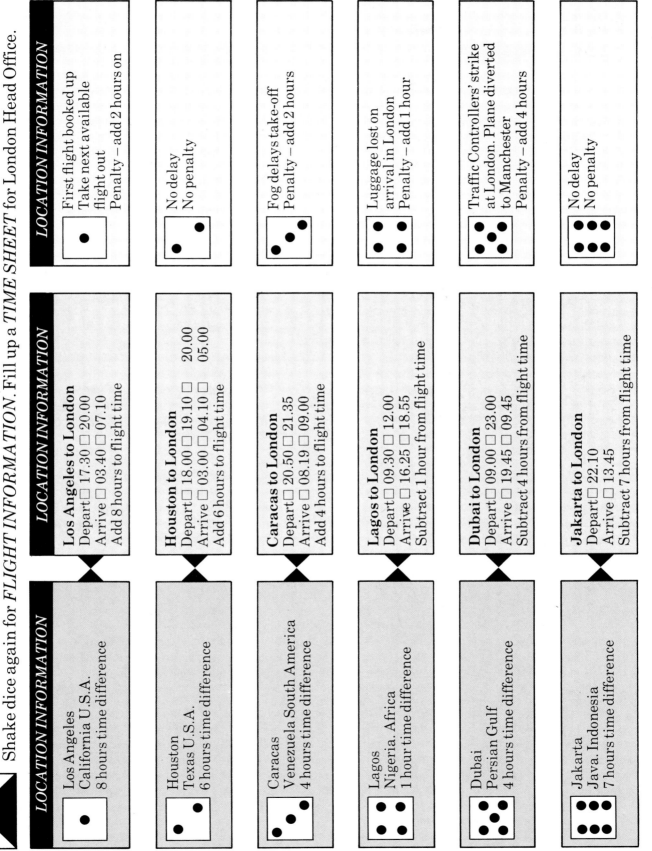

Oil Glossary

anchor handler: supply ship with winch for laying anchors when a semi-submersible is being put in position for drilling.

asphalt: mixture of **bitumen** with small stones or sand. Used for pavements, roofs and road surfaces.

assistant driller: second in charge of drilling operations.

ballast: something heavy used to weigh down a ship and keep it steady when it has no cargo.

barge: large flat vessel that has to be towed.

barrel: (of oil): measure of oil – 159 litres (approx) or 32 gallons (approx). The word goes back to early days when oil was transported in barrels either by horse and cart or on the railroad.

barytes: rock which grinds down to a fine heavy powder. Mixed with drilling mud to increase its weight and help prevent a blow out.

bends: sickness caused by divers coming up too quickly to the surface. Bubbles of gas prevent the blood circulating. Bends are very painful and dangerous, sometimes causing death.

bit: cutting tool that bores a hole. It is at the end of the drill string and rotated by an engine. Different bits are used for drilling through different kinds of rock.

bitumen: a thick and sticky form of petroleum. It is found in places where oil comes to the surface of the ground and dries out in the sun. It is also made at oil refineries.

bitumen pits: large pools of bitumen that are found in many parts of the world, especially in central America, the Middle East, the East Indies and some parts of the United States.

block: area of land or sea in which companies can ask for permisson to drill for oil or gas.

blow out: dangerous uncontrolled eruption of gas or oil from a well.

blow out preventer: valve that helps to prevent a blow out.

buoyancy bottles: air-filled steel bottles that enable a production jacket to float while it is being put in place. Removed and used again.

cap rock: layer of rock above an oilfield that stops the oil escaping to the surface of the ground.

capital cost: amount of money needed to finance a project such as the construction of an oil production platform.

capping: closing a well to prevent the escape of gas or oil.

cargo: goods carried by ship, aircraft or lorry.

casing: steel tubing that stop the sides of a well caving in.

christmas tree: set of valves at the top of an oil well that controls the flow of oil.

consumer: someone who buys something and uses it.

cracking: turning oil or gas into different substances such as plastics.

crude oil: oil before it is refined. When it comes out of the ground it is called *wild* crude; after it leaves the terminal it is called *stabilised* crude – this is what oil tankers carry.

decompression: slow reduction of pressure so that a diver's body gradually gets used to the pressure at the earth's surface. This prevents him getting the bends.

decompression chamber: a cabin on the deck of a diving support vessel in which the diver can live under pressure for a month at a time. Each day the diver goes down to work in a diving bell and comes back at night to sleep. At the end of a month the pressure is slowly reduced so that he can return to life on shore.

derrick: steel tower on a drilling rig that contains a hoist for the drill pipes. It is usually about 40 metres tall – high enough for three pipes (a stand) to be hauled out at the same time.

derrickman: member of the drilling crew who works high up in the derrick and controls the supply of drill pipes.

directional drilling: drilling a well at an angle instead of straight down. This is done so that several holes can be drilled from the same place; they spread out underground and draw oil or gas from a large area.

drill crew: team of people drilling a well. In order of importance they are: drilling superintendent, tool pusher (foreman), driller (controlling the engines), assistant driller, derrick man, roughneck, roustabout

drill pipes: steel tubes about 9 metres long, and screwed together to form a drill string. Made of high quality steel because the drill string may be more than a mile long and have a bend in it when directional drilling is needed.

drilling mud: special mixture of clays, water and chemicals pumped down the well during drilling.

drilling superintendent: person in charge of the drilling crew.

dry well: well that does not find oil or gas.

expand: get bigger.

friction: rubbing one thing against another.

fuel: something burned to produce energy.

gathering station: central point to which crude oil from different onshore wells is brought by pipeline or by tanker.

heavy security harness: straps and hooks that are part of a diver's gear and can be used to lift him if he gets into difficulties.

hyperbaric chamber: any place where the air pressure can be increased. Injured divers can be taken to hospital in small hyperbaric chambers that can be lifted on to helicopters.

industry: business that produces something for sale.

jacket: steel or concrete base on which an offshore production platform stands.

jack-up rig: drilling rig that stands on legs in shallow water. The legs can be jacked up when it is towed to another area.

location: place.

log: record of a ship or aircraft's journeys.

lubricant: substance which reduces friction.

lubricate: make slippery by using oil or water.

modules: ready-made sets of equipment such as gas separation units or living quarters that can quickly and easily be put in position.

mud: see **drilling mud.**

nodding donkey: pump that is used to collect oil from an onshore oilfield.

offshore: out at sea.

offshore installation manager: person in charge of everything that happens on a rig or platform offshore.

oilfield: large area of underground rock that contains oil.

onshore: on land.

peak production: amount of gas or oil produced in the year when production is at its highest.

petroleum: crude oil and what is made from it.

pile: long steel rod driven 50 metres or more into the sea bed to keep a platform in place.

pipes: see **drill pipes.**

pressure: force pressing on to something.

product: something made ready for use or sale.

production facilities: type of structure used to produce oil or gas; for example a platform or subsea module.

production platform: large permanent structure built above an oil well from which oil is sent to the terminal.

pump room: room containing the mud tanks and mud pumps.

radar: television picture that shows where things are even in darkness, fog and mist.

refining: making crude oil ready for use.

recoverable reserves: total amount of oil or gas that a field is expected to produce over its working life.

recovery factor: proportion of oil or gas that seems likely to be recovered from a reservoir.

reserves: total quantity of oil which can be drawn from a well.

reservoir depth: vertical distance between the surface of the land (or of the sea) and the underground reservoir.

reservoir rock: rock that contains oil.

rig: apparatus used to drill wells.

rotary table: wheel lying flat on the drill floor that turns the drill string.

round trip: (a) journey to somewhere and then back again (b) pulling out and replacing the drill string.

roughneck: trained drilling assistant.

roustabout: manual labourer on a drilling rig.

satellite wells: wells in a small oilfield linked to the production platform of a larger oilfield nearby. A christmas tree is fitted on the sea floor and the oil is taken to the platform by a sub-sea pipeline.

semi-submersible: rig that floats on tanks of air. Can move under its own power and drill in deep water even in rough weather.

servicing: checking equipment to make sure it is working properly and replacing worn parts.

spud in: start drilling.

strike: discover a new oilfield.

submersible: made to be used under the water.

sub-sea: underneath the sea.

supply ship: ship which takes supplies out to oil rigs and platforms. It has a flat open cargo deck so that cranes can unload at sea. It also has tanks for transporting water, cement, fuel and drilling mud.

support vessel: barge or ship carrying special equipment to help with work at sea such as diving, repairs or firefighting.

umbilical: line linking a diver with a support vessel. A scuba diver's umbilical is a simple lifeline. The umbilical of deeper divers contains a communications line, an air line, a hot water line and a depth gauge. Also, lines connecting a remotely controlled oil well to the production platform from which it is controlled.

wild cat well: well drilled in search of oil or gas.

wild well: well that has a blow out.

Index

accidents 38, 39
air 4, 8, 30
animals 5, 27
Arctic 26, 27
bends 7
bicycle 29
bit (drilling) 34, 35, 36, 37
boats 18
breathing 8
buoyancy 17
cars 30, 31
communication 10, 11, 14, 15, 39
computer 25, 32
derrick 34
divers 6, 7, 10, 11, 12, 13, 14, 15
diving bell 6, 9
drill 34, 36
drill bit 34, 35, 36, 37
drilling 34, 35, 36, 37
drilling mud 37
drilling rig 19, 24, 27, 34, 35
environment 4, 5, 26, 27
exploration (oil) 32, 33, 34, 35
floating 16, 17, 19
friction 28, 29
gas 32
geologist 32, 33
hand signals 14
jacket 16, 20, 21
lubricant 26, 28, 29, 37
mud 27

North Sea 16, 17, 20, 25, 32
oil 6, 21, 29, 30, 33
oilfield 20, 26, 32
piles 16
pipeline 6, 20, 27
plants 5, 27
plimsoll line 17
pressure 4, 6, 8, 9
production module 25
production 6, 20, 21, 22, 25, 31
rafts 19
rigs 19, 24, 27, 34, 35
rock 32, 33, 34, 47
roughneck 35
rust 30, 31
sea 4, 5, 6, 7
sea bed 5
seismic survey 32, 33
semi-submersible 19
sign language 14
sound 10
strata (rock) 33, 34
strong structures 16, 21
submersibles 6, 7, 10
sunlight 4
support ship 10
telephone 11
umbilical 6, 10
vessels 18
workers 6, 7, 13, 14, 15, 32, 35, 36

First published 1988 by
Ward Lock Educational
47 Marylebone Lane
London W1M 6AX

A member of the Ling Kee Group
LONDON · HONG KONG · NEW YORK
SINGAPORE · TAIPEI

British Library Cataloguing in Publication Data

Solving problems: pupil text for Now!
    project.
    1. Power resources
    I. Doran, H
    333.79   TJ163.2

ISBN 0–7062–4822–8

Designed by Eric Drewery and DP Press
Typeset by DP Press, Sevenoaks, Kent
Printed in Spain by Printeksa, Bilbao

Diagrams DP Press
Illustrators John Plumb 3, 10, 28, 39, 40, 41,
         David Martin 13, 34, 37

Cover photograph Zefa Picture Library

Acknowledgements

The author team, Northern College of Education, Aberdeen,
and Ward Lock Educational Company Limited wish to
acknowledge the outstanding contribution and assistance in
the development of this project that has been provided by
the Occidental North Sea Consortium which comprises:

Occidental Petroleum (Caledonia) Ltd;
Texaco Britain Ltd;
International Thomson Plc;
Union Texas Petroleum Ltd.

We are grateful to the following people for permission to
reproduce the illustrations on the pages listed:

Barnabys Picture Library 3, 18 (three), 30
Ben Odec 24/25
British Petroleum 26, (two), 27 (three)
Carless Exploration 32
Chevron 24/25
Comex Ltd 13
Conoco 24/25
Dundee University 20
Occidental Petroleum (Caledonia) Ltd 5, 6 (three), 16, 18
    (three), 19, 21, 22, 24/25 (three), 31, 35, 36
Royal National Institute for the Deaf 15
Shell UK 24/25, 33
Submex Ltd 12, 13